PLC 102

SEQUENCER

PLC 102

*

* ISBN-13:
* 978-1494356903

*

* ISBN-10:
* 1494356902

*

*

* Brian Daniel Starr is the owners of this work with all rights and responsibilities related to this work.

*

* Copyright 2013 Brian Daniel Starr

*

* All Rights Reserved. No part of this book may be reproduced in any form without permission in writing from the author, except in the case of brief quotations embodied in critical articles or reviews.

*

* Printed in the United States of America

Sequencer Definition

- Sequences thru steps that both have an action when active and have a transistion when complete

- Each step will trigger the action or event

- The Action or event will end with for Example a sensor or a timer finishing

PICK and PLACE

- The pick and place mechanism is a device to show how a sequencer works

- The mechanism will consist of three cylinders actuated by air.

- 1   Close/open clamp

- 2   Travel Up/Down

- 3   Travel In/Out

Transistions

- Clamps are difficult to put sensors on so we will use a timer to say the clamp has actuated

- The Up Down Cylinder will have a sensor that says the Cylinder is Up and a sensor that says the Cylinder is Down

- The In Out Cylinder will have a sensor that says the Cylinder is out or the Cylinder is in

Concept for Pick Place

- The mechanism will go down and PICK up the part
- The mechanism will go up
- The mechanism will go out over the place point
- The mechanism will go down
- The mcahnism will open and PLACE the part on the Place point, then will return

Return Path

- The Return Path is to go up after leaving the part at the PLACE point

- After up the mechanism goes In

- After it is in it waits above the PICK point until it is time or get another part

- Or in some cases it saves time to go down and PICK the part, and then Go Up and wait

- In this example we will wait with an empty clamp

Making Variables or Tags

- We will need a few Registers for the Inputs, Outputs, Timers, and Variables or Tags

- Up will be Input I:1.0

- Down will be Input I:1.1

- In will be Input I:1.2

- Out will be Input I:1.3

- The Register will be an integer register and will be called Step

The Outputs will be single Acting

- There are three Cylinders.   These will have one output for ON and extend and if Off will retract

- The Outputs will be O:1.0 for clamp (grip is on)

- O:1.1 for Down, and off for Up

- O:1.2 for Out and off for In

- Thus if all off the Grip is open Up and In.

Note on Tags

- Older PLC did not have tags that are created and used registers directly

- For this example we will use RS Logix 5000 for the programming so we can use any names for the tags

- We will use the Tags that are the Input and Output Tag Registers so the training will work as well with the Older SLC 500 and PLC 5

List of Tags Used

- I:1.0, I:1.1,I:1.2,I:1.3,O:1.0,O:1.1,O:1.2, Timer1, Timer2, Step

- Cooresponding to these tags is the following list

- Up, Down, In, Out, Clamp, Down, Out

Steps Defined

- Step 0   Wait
- Step 1   Go Down
- Step 2   Clamp
- Step 3   Go Up
- Step 4   Go Out
- Step 5   Go Down
- Step 6   Release Clamp
- Step 7   Go Up
- Step 8   Go In

Step 0

Wait for Cycle On Switch
Progress to Step 1
I:1.4 Cycle On
Local:1:I.Data.4
EQU
Equal
Source A   STEP
0
Source B   0
MOV
Move
Source   1   Dest   STEP
0

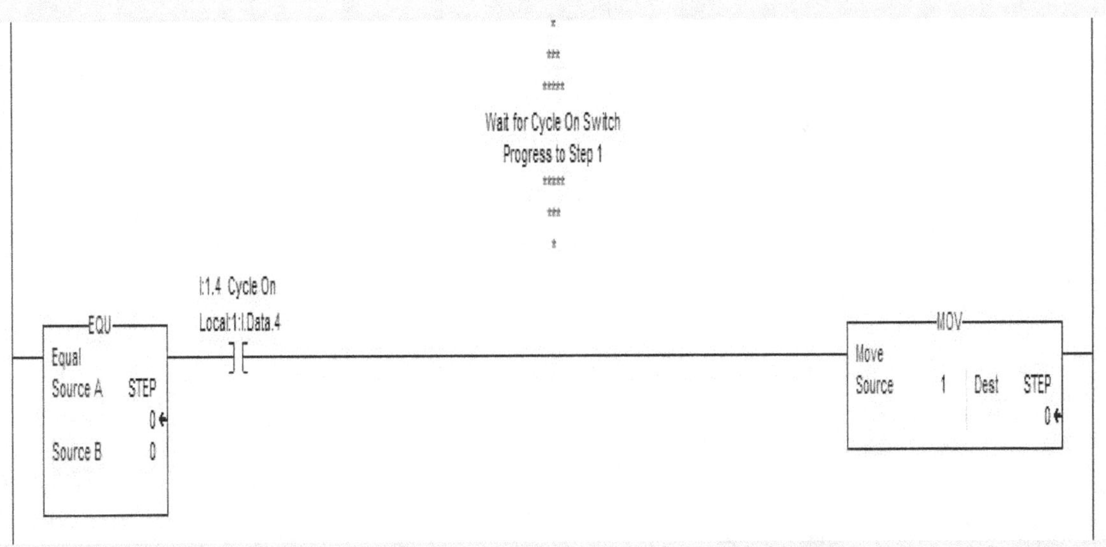

Step 1

Send Clamp Down and Wait For Sensor
Progress to Step 2

I:1.0 Cylinder One
is Down
Local:1:I.Data.0

EQU
Equal
Source A   STEP
0
Source B   1

MOV
Move
Source   2   Dest   STEP
0

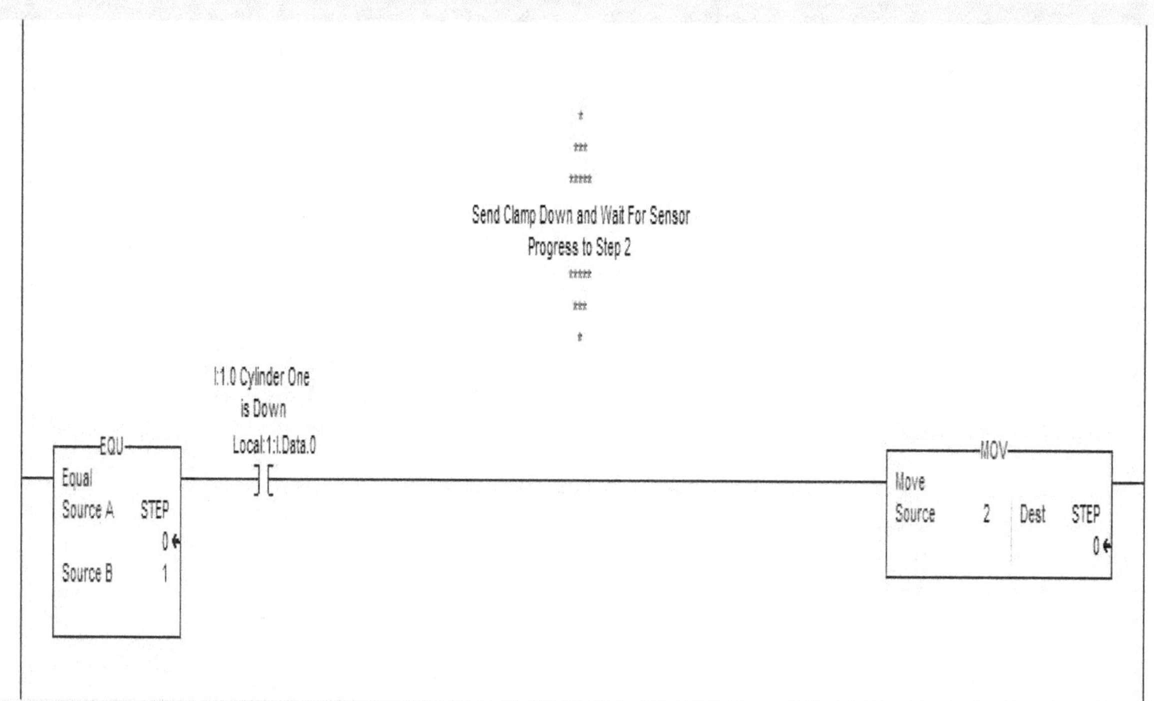

Step 2

Close Clamp, Wait for Timer that assumes Clamp is Closed
Progress to Step 3

2
EQU
Equal
Source A   STEP
0
Source B   2
TIMER1.DN
MOV
Move
Source   3   Dest   STEP
0

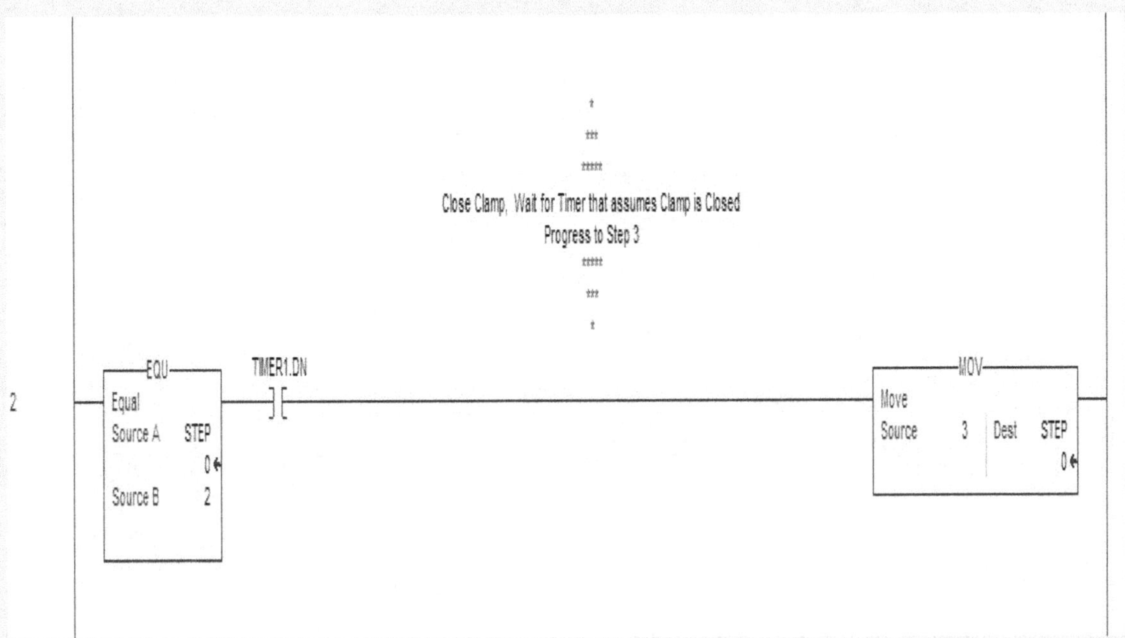

Step 3

*
***
*****
Send Clamp Up with Payload, Wait for Up Sensor
Progress to Step 4
*****
***
*

I:1.1 Cylinder One
is Up
Local:1:I.Data.1

EQU
Equal
Source A   STEP
0
Source B   3

MOV
Move
Source   4   Dest   STEP
0

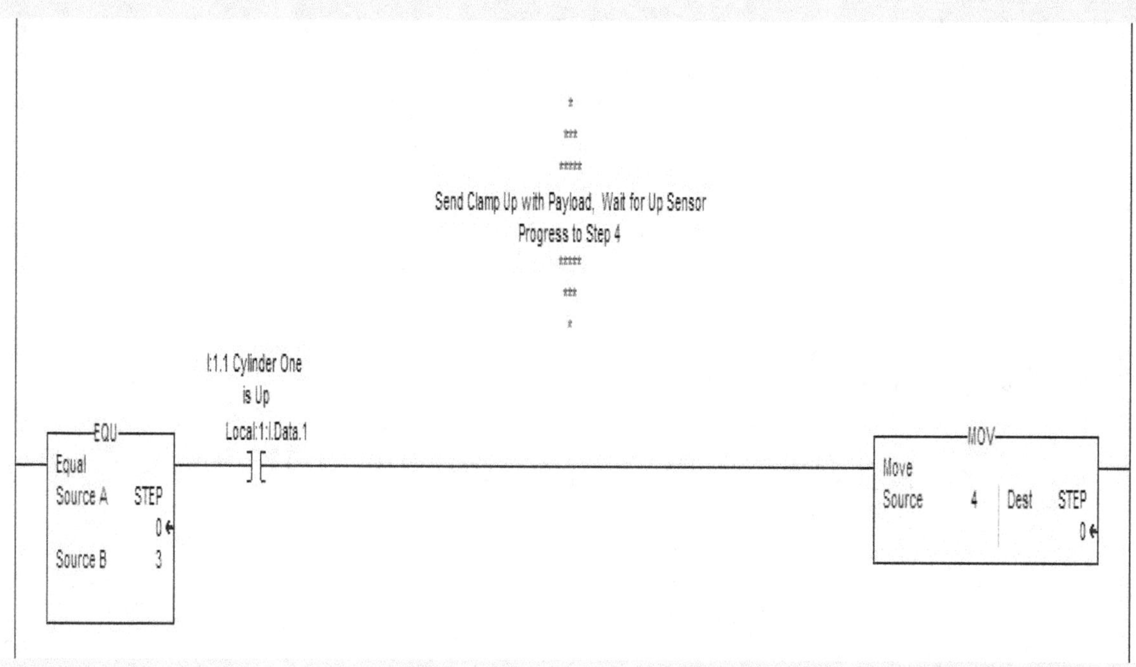

Step 4

*
***
*****
Send Cylinder Out with Payload, Wait for Sensor Cylinder Out
Progress to Step 5
*****
***
*

I:1.2 Cylinder Two
is Out
Local:1:I.Data.2

EQU
Equal
Source A   STEP
0
Source B   4

MOV
Move
Source   5   Dest   STEP
0

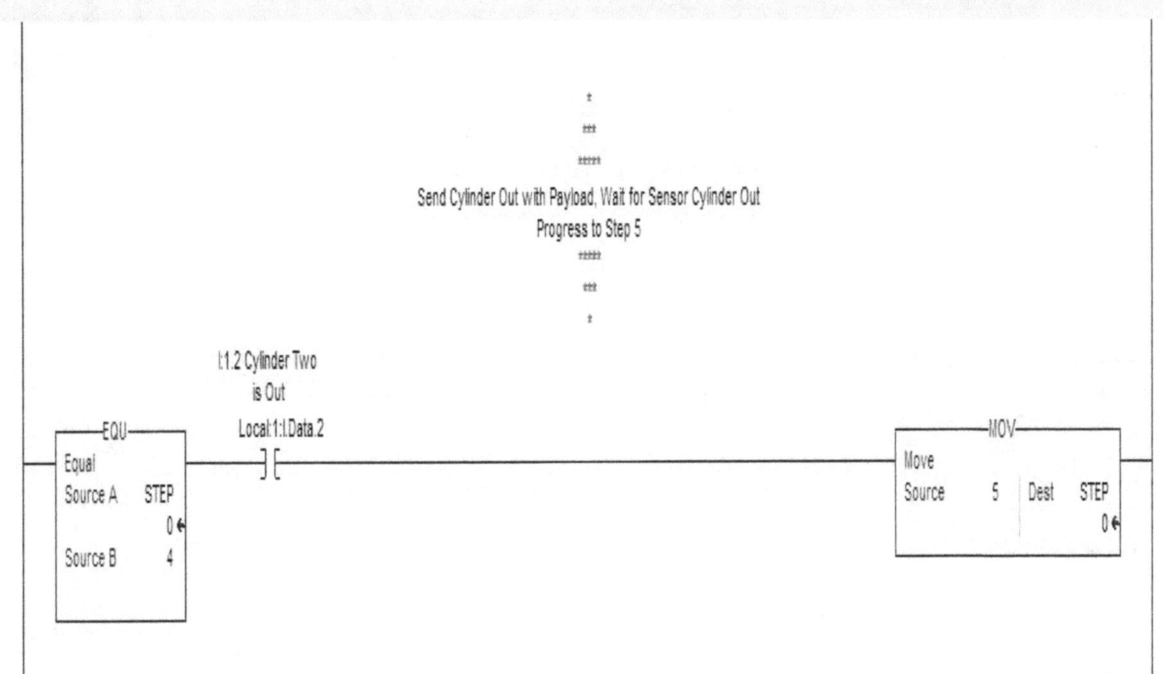

Step 5

*
***
*****
Send cylinder Down with Payload over Place Point, Wait for Sensor Cylinder is Down
Progress to Step 6
*****
***
*

I:1.0 Cylinder One
is Down
Local:1:I.Data.0

EQU
Equal
Source A   STEP
0
Source B   5

MOV
Move
Source   6   Dest   STEP
0

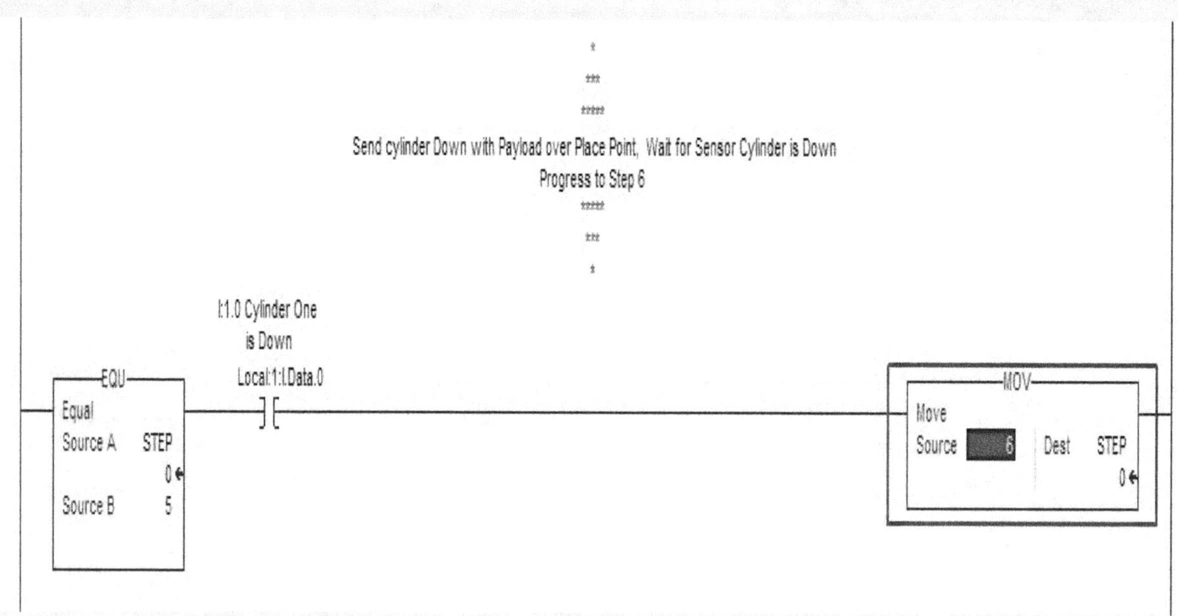

Step 6

*
***
*****
Unclamp and release Payload on Place Point, Wait for Timer to expire saying Clamp Open
Progress to Step 7
*****
***
*

EQU
Equal
Source A   STEP
                   0
Source B   6

TIMER2.DN

MOV
Move
Source   7   Dest   STEP
                                       0

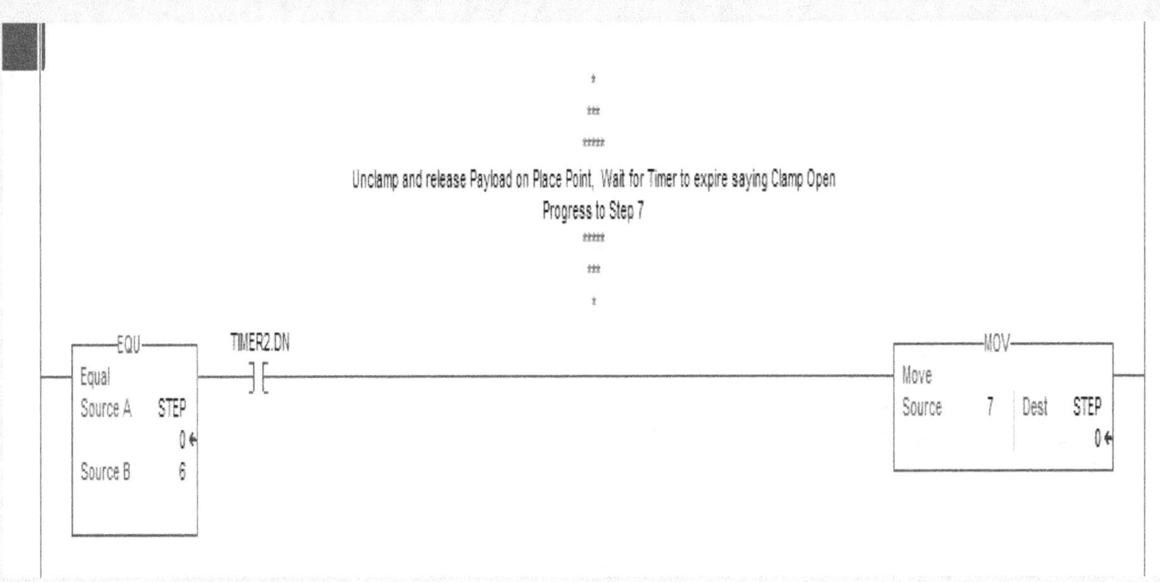

Step 7

*
***
*****
Send Cylinder Up, Wait for Sensor to Come Up
Progress to Step 8
*****
***
*

I:1.1 Cylinder One
is Up
Local:1:I.Data.1

EQU
Equal
Source A   STEP
                0
Source B   7

MOV
Move
Source   8   Dest   STEP
                                   0

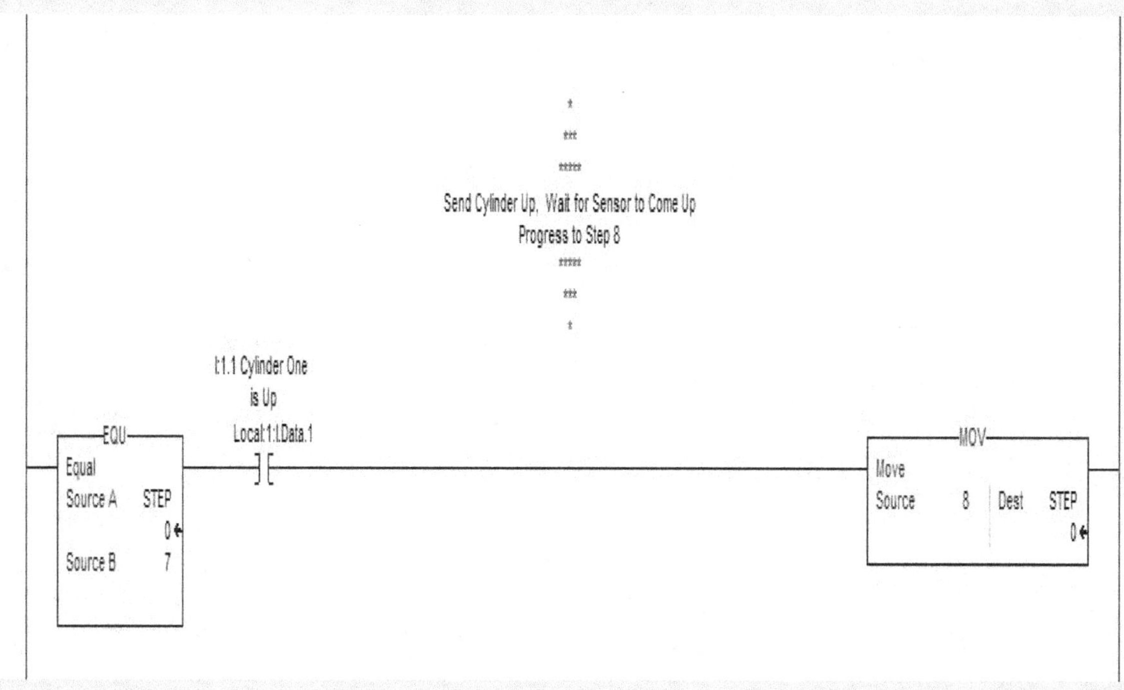

Step 8

Send Cylinder In, Wait for Sensor that Cylinder is In
Progress to Step 0
I:1.3 Cylinder Two
is In
Local:1:I.Data.3
EQU
Equal
Source A   STEP
0
Source B   8
MOV
Move
Source   0   Dest   STEP
0

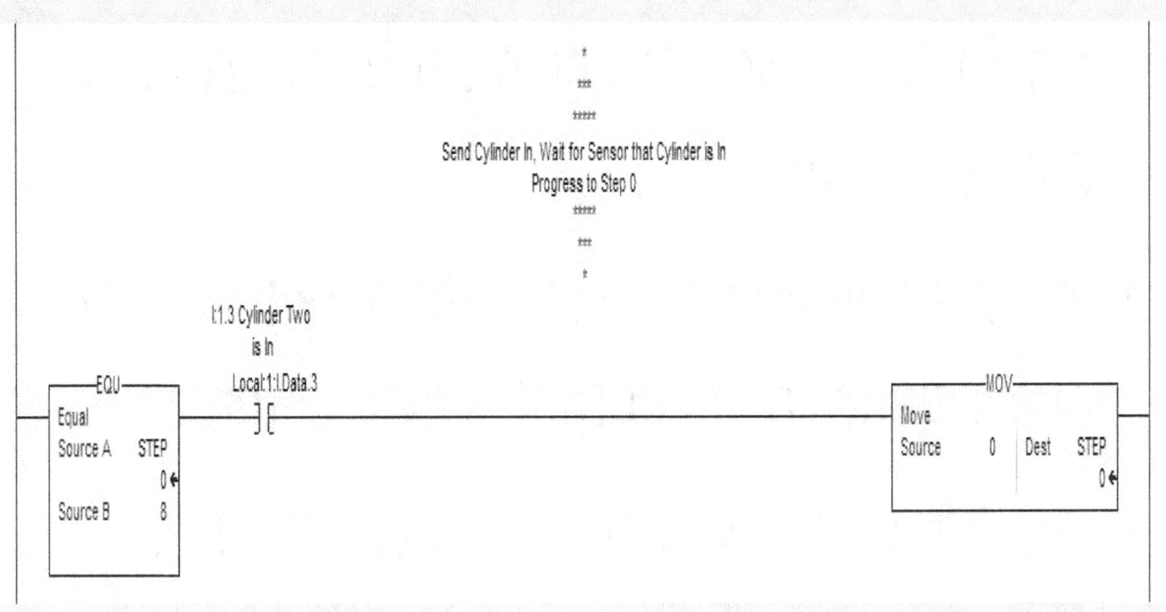

Actions

- For Each Step something must be actuated or a timer started

- In PLC programming it is customary that only one instance of an output is ever entered

- In other words, you cannot have the same output in two places

- Thus if an output such as Down is in more than one place there are two conditions to make it work.

Actions Continued

- Also if the action is to be out for more than one step the output must have more than one step to actuate the output

- Because the output coil is only entered in one place the steps are entered in parallel on the rung

Clamp

*****
For Steps 2,3,4,5, Hold Clamp On (Closed on Payload)
*****
***
*
9
O:2.0 Clamp
Local:2:O.Data.0
( )
EQU
Equal
Source A   STEP
0
Source B   2
EQU
Equal
Source A   STEP
0
Source B   3
EQU
Equal
Source A   STEP
0
Source B   4
EQU
Equal
Source A   STEP
0
Source B   5

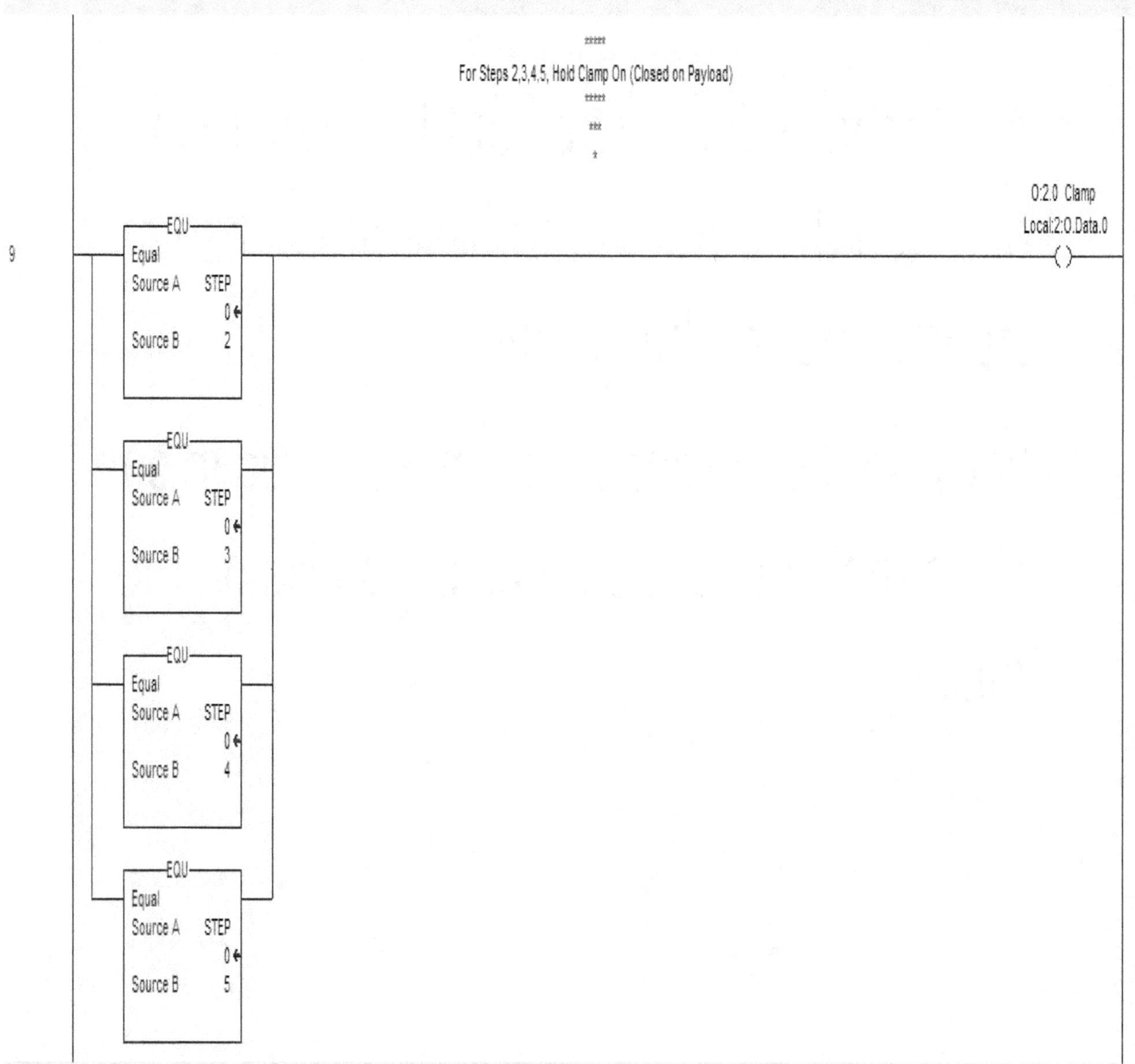

Down

Extend Cylinder Down for Steps 1,2, and 5,6

10

EQU
Equal
Source A   STEP
                0
Source B   1

EQU
Equal
Source A   STEP
                0
Source B   2

EQU
Equal
Source A   STEP
                0
Source B   5

EQU
Equal
Source A   STEP
                0
Source B   6

O:2.1 Down
Local:2:O.Data.1
( )

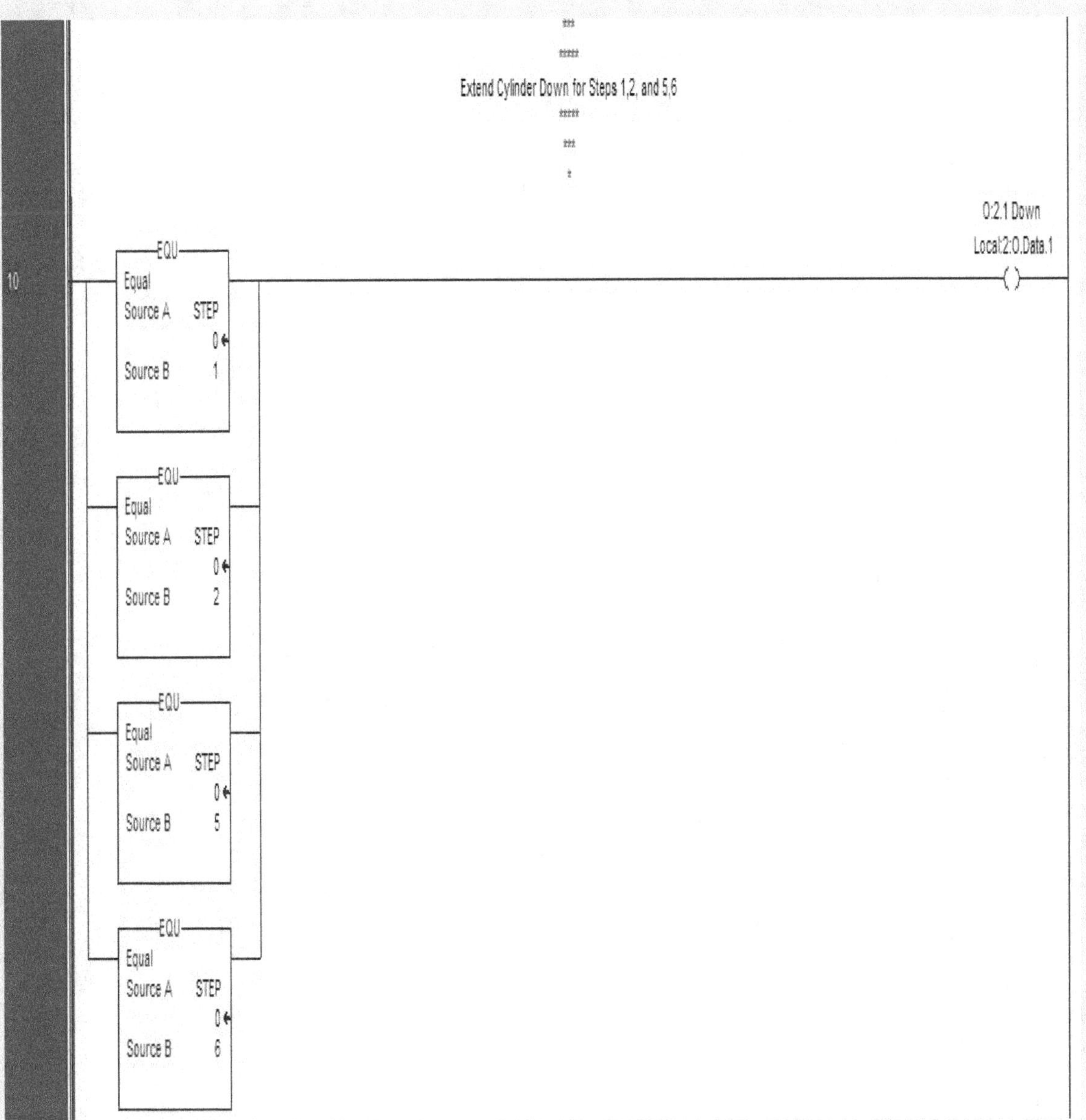

Out

Extend Cyclinder Out for Steps 4,5,6,7
11
EQU
Equal
Source A   STEP
0
Source B   4
EQU
Equal
Source A   STEP
0
Source B   5
EQU
Equal
Source A   STEP
0
Source B   6
EQU
Equal
Source A   STEP
0
Source B   7
O:2.1 Out
Local:2:O.Data.2

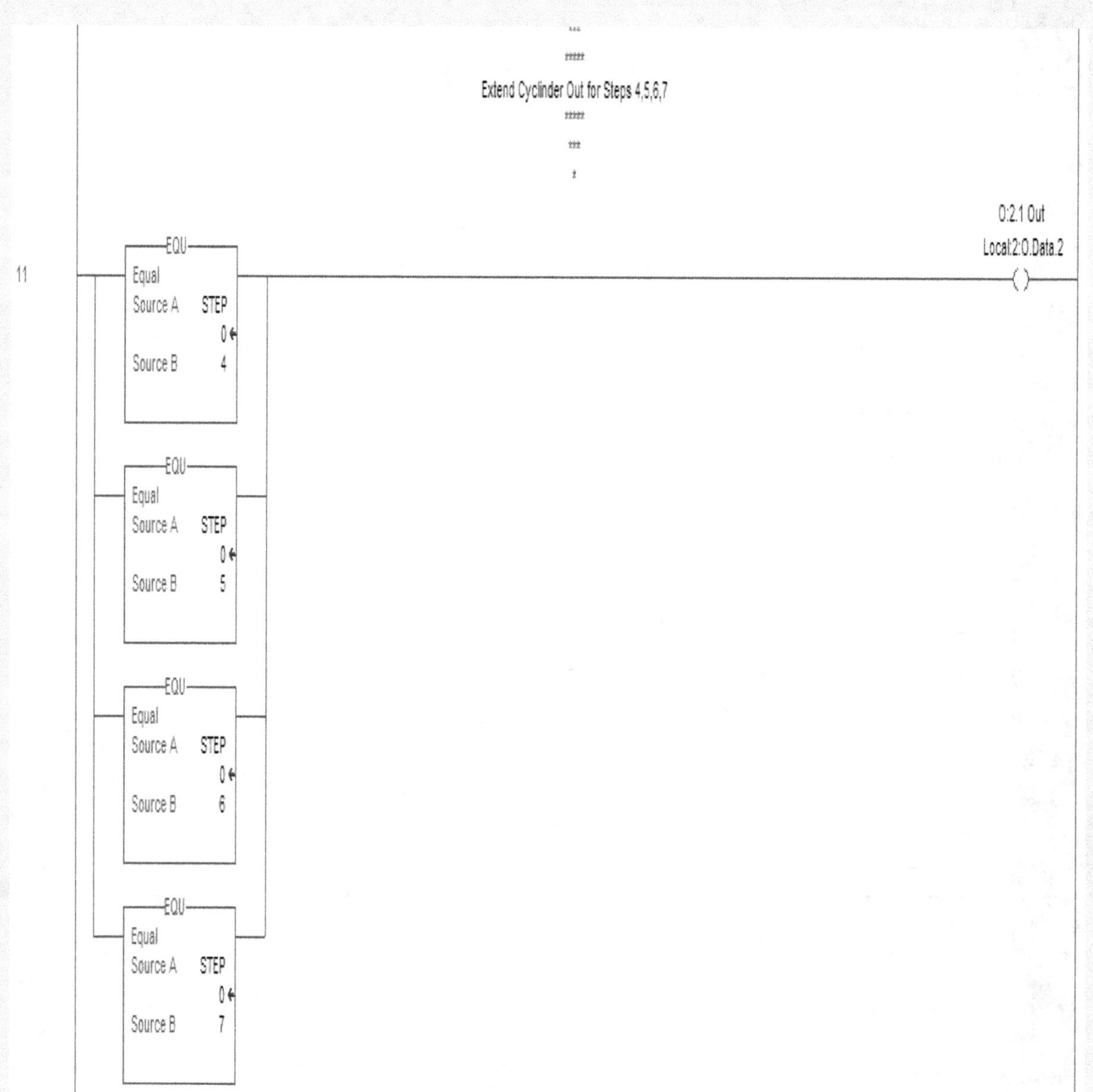

Timer One

Timer One is on for one half second (500 miliseconds) for Clamp to close
EQU
Equal
Source A   STEP
0
Source B   2
TON
Timer On Delay   (EN)
Timer   TIMER1   (DN)
Preset   500
Accum   0
12

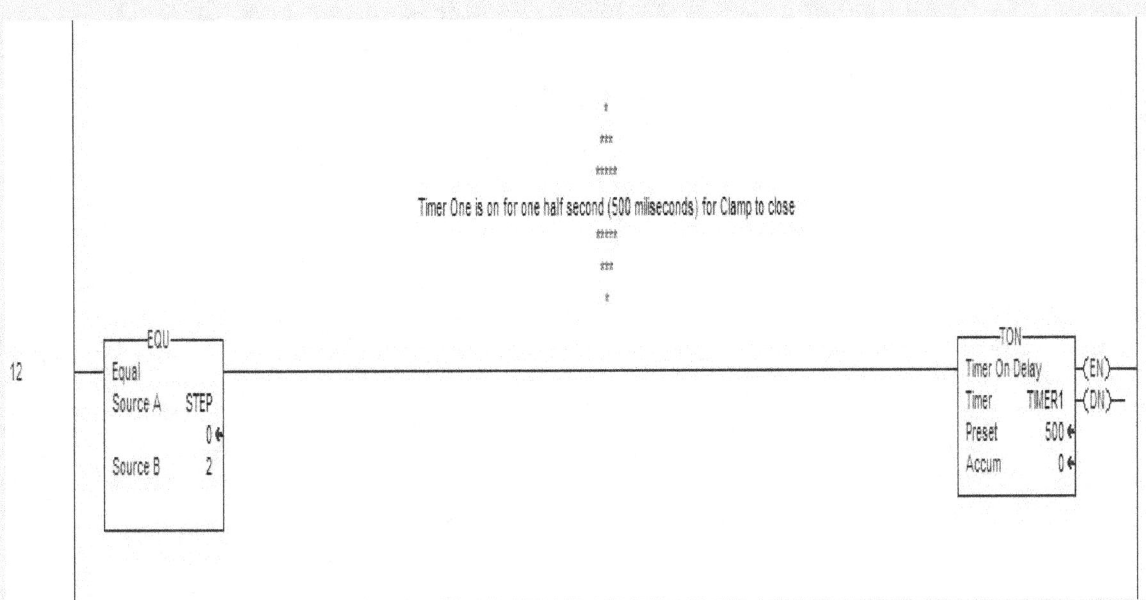

Timer Two

*
***
*****
Timer Two is on for one half second for Clamp to Open
*****
***
*

EQU
Equal
Source A   STEP
                  0
Source B   5

TON
Timer On Delay   —(EN)—
Timer   TIMER2   —(DN)—
Preset   500
Accum   0

13

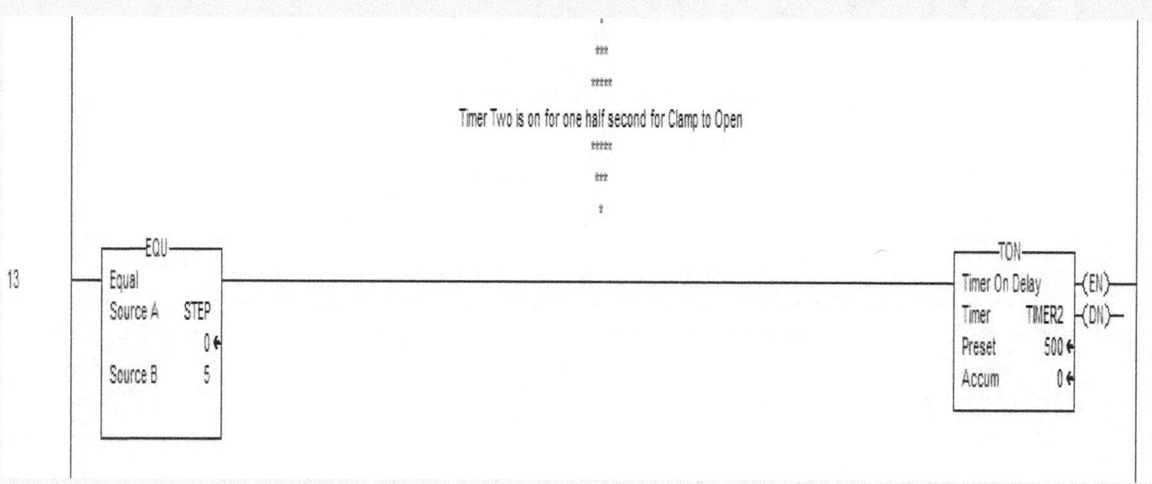

Notice All Steps Not Used

- Because the cyclinders return when they are not on, the steps 3 and 7 are go Up or turn off the Down, the steps 8 are go In or turn off the Out and the steps 6 are unclamp or turn off the clamp.

Contact for Cycle On

- This contact is the contact for step 0 to go to step 1

- If this contact copied to every step then the process can be stopped at any step by opening the Cycle On contact

Typical Pick and Place

- The Pick and Place is a basic building block of machine control

- A Machine will usually have a few pick and place and then an operation to put the parts together

- A Pick and Place can be used for picking up parts and putting on a machine as well as picking up parts from the machine and putting them in output bin off machine.

Many Station Machine

- A machine will have a sequencer for each station on a machine

- A sequencer will be triggered as well for turning the table on a machine

- Each pick and place fills a station, then the table rotates and it does it again

- A 25 station machine will cycle 25 times before a complete part is made, but then everytime it cycles it makes a new part.